HUSBANDS

AN OWNER'S MANUAL

HOW TO SURVIVE A 50-YEAR MARRIAGE

Judi Schindler

Husbands: An Owner's Manual
How to Survive a 50-Year Marriage

Cover and book design by Mike Wykowski, www.mawmaw.net
Cover illustrations by Elwood H. Smith, copyright © 2011 Elwood H. Smith
Additional illustrations by Mike Wykowski

ISBN 978-0-692-95702-8
BISAC: Humor / Topic / Men, Women & Relationaships

Visit the author at www.judischindler.com

FOREWORD

When I was a 22-year-old newlywed, I thought it was my job to come home every day from work and prepare my bridegroom a proper dinner of salad, meat, potatoes and vegetables. (This was the '60s after all.)

Every night I dutifully brought forth a two- or three-course meal, which my new husband would immediately reject. I discovered he didn't like meat that had been frozen; he didn't like leftovers; he didn't like casseroles. The list went on. One thing he did like, however, was veal parmesan. Couldn't I make that?

So one day I found a recipe. I bought the veal, pounded the veal, breaded the veal and sautéed it. I made two sauces. From scratch. I grated the cheese. That evening, I presented my day's efforts to my husband in triumph. I was expecting words of surprise, delight and gratitude or, at the very least, a pat on the head. Instead, he said:

"Oh . . . I forgot to tell you. I don't like veal parmesan anymore."

As God is my witness, he never tasted it . . . never even lifted his fork.

Fifty years later, I am still married to that man. I don't cook for him anymore, of course. (I'm not insane.) But we're still married.

INTRODUCTION

Back in the Middle Ages, couples didn't divorce. They didn't have to. Famine and disease put them out of their misery.

But today, a 25-year-old bride or groom can expect to live to at least 80. That's 55 years or more of togetherness. So without the benefit of the Bubonic Plague, it's no surprise that 50 percent of first-time marriages break up. For second marriages, the break-up rate is 64%. And for third marriages, it's 76%.

(They say that insanity is defined by doing the same thing over and over and expecting a different result each time.)

As someone who has been married for more than 50 years, I can attest to the fact that even nice guys are hard to live with.

You remember Marlo Thomas – "That Girl," "Free to Be You and Me." (If you're under 40, Google it.) Marlo has been married to former talk-show host Phil Donahue since 1980. If you ever saw his show, you know that Phil Donahue is a warm, funny, sensitive guy – very sensitive.

Marlo Thomas says, "Phil Donahue is the best husband in the whole world, and he's not all that great."

Given that husbands aren't easy, it seems to me they should come with instruction manuals – just like washing machines and digital cameras. There are instruction manuals for toasters, for God's sake.

A while back, the cartoon strip "Hagar the Horrible" depicted Helga, his long-suffering wife, praying to the heavens with this lament:

"When I was young, I asked you to send me a husband. You did, and I'm grateful."

In the next frame she adds, "But is it too late to ask for the instruction manual?"

If you agree with Helga and me that a husband should come with a manual, the question is: Who should write it? We've heard from the psychologists, marriage counselors and sex therapists. They all talk the talk. The real experts are those of us who've put up with a man who won't eat veal parmesan, and other indignities, for 50 years or more.

Let me take a moment to describe my credentials. That would be Jack Schindler, the love of my life. He's tall, good-looking and very sweet – I'd even say nurturing. If I'm driving to the suburbs, he fills the car with gas. If I'm sick, he makes me soup. He shovels the walk without being asked, and he does all the grocery shopping.

But, like Phil Donahue, he does have issues:

Food Issues

He won't eat anything I make. (It turns out veal parmesan wasn't the only problem.)

Time Issues

He has to be early wherever we go.

Cultural Issues

He only likes movies where things blow up or there's a car chase and very little dialogue. (Grunting is OK, but no talking).

Tidiness Issue

He throws his clothes on the floor and leaves used toothpicks all over the house.

Personality Issues

And oh yes, he's just a tiny bit passive aggressive. (If we disagree, he sighs and walks out of the room.)

After 50 years, I think I know a thing or two about selecting a husband and operating him in good working order, all of which I've documented in the following pages. I dedicate this manual to Helga and any other woman who would like to stay married for the rest of her life.

CHAPTER 1

SAMPLING THE MERCHANDISE

Never live with a man you don't intend to marry.

Please note, I didn't say, "Don't have sex before marriage." I didn't even say, "Never live with a man before marriage." I merely wish to point out that most men make lousy roommates. Gay men being the possible exception.

I admit that hetero-male roommates have a few benefits as well. They can change light bulbs, take out the garbage and massage your neck or libido as you prefer. But actually living with a hetero man means stepping over dirty underwear and losing all rights to the remote control. Why would you do that unless you intend to get half his net worth some day?

The ideal situation may be a part-time, live-in boyfriend.

I have a friend who found a winning formula. Katie has been dating Dave for 11 years. They travel together a few times a year, and he stays at her place on the weekends. Katie says that all the women in her building (most of whom are in their 50s) have come to her, one by one, asking how they might send their husbands home with Dave on Monday and have them return on Friday. One gentleman also inquired if Dave would take his wife.

Long-distance marriages have a similar advantage.

When they first met, Jennifer lived in Indianapolis, Nat in Chicago. After a year of correspondence, Jennifer invited Nat to Indianapolis for the Indy 500. Then Nat

Benefits of Living with a Gay Man:

1. You can borrow his clothes.

2. He'll tell you truthfully if your ass looks fat.

3. He'll dress appropriately as your plus-one to weddings and holiday parties.

4. He'll clean out the kitchen of all but fat-free foods. (OK, you can have a scoop of Haagen Dazs on special occasions -- like Liza Minelli's birthday.)

5. He can perform a simple mani-pedi in a pinch.

countered with a weekend in Chicago. The following weekend, they were engaged and a year later they got married. That was 20 years ago.

Jennifer still lives in Indianapolis, Nat in Chicago. A long-distance romance became a long-distance marriage. They think it's great. They spend Monday through Friday alone, in sweats, doing laundry, cleaning, shopping and paying bills, all the mundane tasks. She eats cereal for dinner watching Downton Abbey reruns. He farts at will. Their weekends are for fun, sex, bonding and conversation. They don't seem to mind that it means makeup for her and sphincter control for him.

"From the time we say hello until the time we say goodbye, it's like a wonderful date," he says. Each always brings the other a little surprise. "It might be a book or a picture or flowers or something practical like a kitchen utensil," Nat says. And when it comes to Christmas and birthdays they go all out. "We work our buns off to make them special."

Back when I was dating (sometime between the invention of the Model T and the microwave), a young lady might receive a friendship ring or a fraternity pin as a symbol of pre-engagement. Today, young couples seem to hire a U-Haul to signify the same thing. Let me assure you, it's a lot easier to return a fraternity pin than it is to divide up a household and break a lease.

Relationship experts often advise against cohabiting *especially* if you want to get married. Debra Macleod, who writes for the *The Huffington Post*, points out that living together "removes much of a man's motivation to make the formal commitment of marriage within a reasonable time." She also points out that the live-in boyfriend no longer has to pursue his girlfriend. "And if something is too easily acquired, it just doesn't hold the same value as something that's more challenging."

In other words, your mother was right. "Why buy the organic cow if you can get the soy-milk latte for free?"

Now here are a few reasons why being married is better than living together:

For starters, there's more incentive to overlook annoying behavior (yours as well as his), not to mention petty arguments and forgotten birthdays. Every long-term marriage has survived more than a few slammed doors. I have friends who recently celebrated 50 years of happy marriage. They were actually married 52 years, but the first two were a living hell.

Then there's the issue of procreation. If you want children, it's probably better for them if you're married – fewer awkward moments in the playground and at parent-teacher conferences.

And don't kid yourself; a break-up between live-ins can be just as messy and expensive as a full-blown divorce.

> **To sum it up, cohabitation may look like marriage without the paperwork, but it lacks the financial advantages, social approval and long-term security.**

Minus those benefits, there's no reason to put up with:

a.   someone else's hair in the bathroom sink

b.   a damp jock strap on the bed

c.   an empty toilet paper roll

d.   someone else's mother.

CHAPTER 2

PRODUCT COMPARISON

There's a wide variety of potential husbands on the market – each with different features and different limitations. Unfortunately, you can't get everything you want in one model.

It's like buying a car. You walk into the showroom, and over here you have your minivans. Roomy, yes; functional, very; but they scream fries on the floor, hockey sticks in the way back and Tums in the glove compartment. You can just see yourself driving your kids to school, still in your pajamas, with a mocha latte double espresso between your knees and your cell phone cradled on your shoulder.

On the opposite side of the showroom are your sports cars – completely impractical, terrible mileage, expensive to repair and totally uncomfortable. But also fast, flashy and sexy. You can envision yourself speeding along some twisty road on the French Riviera or Amalfi Coast, top down, wind in your hair and a hot guy in the passenger seat.

Maybe you're attracted to one of those big, brawny SUVs that would be a nightmare to park. Or you're pining for a luxury sedan with heated leather seats and a price tag approximating Ivanka Trump's annual wardrobe budget. Diesels, hybrids – what is it that gets your motor racing?

Let's kick some tires, compare features and see if there's a potential husband that's a good fit for you. Here are a few of the more popular models you're likely to encounter.

Goodtime Charlie

You know Charlie – he's effervescent, enthusiastic and energetic. He's the life of the party, a great dancer, outgoing and lots of fun. You couldn't ask for a better playmate. Want to try a new restaurant? Charlie's there. A party? Of course. Clubbing? Do you have to ask?

Product Limitations!

Need I remind you of Charlie Sheen? Admittedly, Sheen is an extreme example (although he seems to have cleaned up his act since his tiger blood days). But even the best of Charlies are better in good times than hard times. When the music stops, they're likely to sulk or bail. And if someone gets sick, don't expect Charlie to whip up a batch of chicken soup.

The Guy-Guy

The guy-guy is all man. He likes meat and potatoes, cold beer and spectator sports. He is loyal, trustworthy and not likely to wander too far off the couch.

While he may not be much of a playmate, the guy-guy is a pretty great helpmate. ('Cause that's what guys do.) When the baby is crying at 3 a.m., you're suffering from an abscessed tooth and the bathtub is leaking through to the floor below, you'll be glad you married this guy.*

* The previous sentence aptly describes 22% of married life.

Product Limitations!

He won't eat anything he didn't try before he was 12. He falls asleep at the symphony and foreign films. And he won't give up his stonewashed jeans.

The High-Powered Executive

Who hasn't admired the captain of industry . . . the Wall Street magnate . . . the media mogul – Steve Jobs, Daymond John, Gordon Gecko or (my personal favorite) Don Draper. He battled his way to the top, stepping over the competition and working incredibly long hours. Now he's made it. He has the corner office, the cushy salary. And he can buy you anything you want, Little Lady. All you have to do is look perfect, throw perfect dinner parties and raise perfect children. Is that too much to ask?

Product Limitations!

Several years ago, Fortune Magazine ran an article about the CEO of Sony, who said at a company meeting, "I don't see my family much. My family is you." Great for the company; not so great for his wife and kids.

A workaholic is a workaholic. They can't turn it off just because they've succeeded. You can expect to come in second . . . for the rest of your life.

Mr. Fixit

Wouldn't you like to have this guy around? No more closet doors that don't close, loose floorboards or leaky faucets. Mr. Fixit has all the right tools, and he knows how to use them. He can install a toilet and rewire a lamp. He can even put up drywall. For those who have come to believe that all repair jobs begin and end with duct tape, this can be very appealing.

Product Limitations!

As good as he is at putting things together, Mr. Fixit is also pretty good at taking them apart – and leaving them spread out across your dining-room floor. Mrs. Fixit is thus condemned to live in a never-ending construction site.

Don't worry, he'll put it all back together. When? When he buys that new tool or finds a replacement for that broken part. (Yeah, right.)

The Nerd

Nerds are worth looking into. For starters, they're usually a lot nicer than cooler dudes, and they're more likely to appreciate female attention.

The thing you should know about nerds, however, is they suffer from a mild-to-severe case of obsessive-compulsive disorder. They immerse themselves in one topic and are virtually oblivious to anything else around them.

Typically, nerds are supposed to obsess about Star Trek or computer games. But, in my experience, there are also golf nerds, bird-watching nerds, fishing nerds, music nerds and marathon runners. And don't forget those Civil War re-enactors.

Rachel is married to another category of nerd – an amateur magician. Bert, her husband, has spent tens of thousands of dollars on magic tricks, which have taken over their spare bedroom. The pride of the collection is a custom-made box for sawing a woman in half. (It should be pointed out that Bert has never performed this trick, because he can't persuade Rachel or anyone else to get into the box.)

Product Limitations!

His nerdy obsession is going to take up a lot of time and money – not to mention your house. Plan to spend a lot of vacations at Star Trek conventions and Civil War battle sites.

!!CONSUMER PRODUCT ALERT!!

This book is temporarily interrupted
with the following special announcement.

NEVER GET INVOLVED WITH A PROFESSIONAL ATHLETE

Two words of caution: "Tiger Woods."

And I don't blame Tiger. It's not his fault. Every professional athlete was once a remarkably gifted child. From the time he could lift a bat, dribble a ball or swing a club, he was treated like a little god. The older he got, the more he was adored, fawned over and worshipped. Girls threw themselves at him. Men just wanted to hang around him. In college, he got excused from tests and was given better food than other students. It is a fact: Professional athletes get away with murder, sometimes literally (O.J. Simpson).

Rock stars, by contrast, struggle for years before they get that kind of adulation – except, of course, Justin Bieber, who, I think we can agree, would not make good marriage material either.

Athletes grow up being worshipped. It's become part of their DNA. And there isn't a woman on earth who can satisfy that kind of ego.

Do you remember when Alex Rodriguez dumped Cameron Diaz, for Pete's sake?

Just keep this in mind: Professional athletes may be rich and handsome and lead lavish lives of celebrity, but too much adoration too young is impossible to overcome.

~~~~~~~~~~

OK. We've looked at some of the product types out there. And, of course, this is just a small sample. You also have your dashing ladykiller (George Clooney), your boyish charmer (Hugh Grant), your eccentric billionaire (Warren Buffet), cheaters (Bill Clinton) and *assholes* (Kanye West).

Then there are the hybrids. (A little of this, a little of that.)

The point is none of them is perfect. For every shiny, chrome-plated hubcap, there's a tiny ping in the engine. You need to understand both before taking full possession.

CHAPTER 3

NEW VS. OLDER MODELS

I'm not sure when it happened, but sometime in the last 20 to 25 years, the factory began producing a newer line of men.

These new models come equipped with some decided advantages over the older models. They're a little more sensitive, a little more evolved. (They dress better, groom better and are more open-minded when your niece becomes your nephew.)

The new models actually change diapers, weep openly at sad movies and (miraculously) do laundry.

The older models (the kind I am more familiar with) can't be trusted anywhere near the temperature settings of a washer or dryer. I used to think the best way to tell if a man was really single was by his wrinkled shirt and the ironic pink tint of his sweat socks. All that's changed. My own son, for example, does the laundry at his house.

The difference between the two generations can be attributed to the way they grew up. Older men are more likely to have had a stay-at-home mom who did all the cooking and cleaning. Most younger men had working mothers, so they were forced to learn a few domestic skills if they didn't want to walk around naked and hungry.

It should be noted that while younger men offer a few upgraded product features their fathers lacked, they do have a few defects of their own. For starters, your average millennial will never run around the car to open a door for a woman or stand up when she enters the room. You have as much chance getting him to help you with your coat as having him shave that annoying goatee. And, I can tell you from personal experience, none of them will offer an old lady a seat on the bus. *(Hey, young man staring at your phone, I know you saw me!)*

While younger men may lack the chivalry gene, they do have compensating factors worth considering. They have the energy and sensitivity, which, in theory, should make them better lovers. (Feel free to take a test-drive and make up your own mind.)

My friend Melissa says she once had a boyfriend who was 17 years older. Her next boyfriend was 17 years younger. The older boyfriend took her on trips and to nice restaurants, but he turned out to be a little controlling.

The deathblow was delivered the night she prepared a dinner party for him and four of his friends. He insisted on accompanying her to the grocery store to shop for the meal. Every time she put something in the cart, he put it back on the shelf.

Her selections were "too big," "too expensive" or "the wrong brand." Later, when he went out to play golf, she drove back to the store, bought what she needed and planned her escape.

In retrospect, Melissa preferred the energy of the younger boyfriend both inside and outside the bedroom. So much so, she didn't mind picking up the tab for nice trips and fancy restaurants herself.

If, like Melissa, you decide to cross the generation dating gap, you may encounter a few incompatabilities.

1. One of you thinks a "church key" is something that opens a chapel door. The other thinks a "hook up" means getting your telephone installed.

2. One of you has no idea what "Beta Max" means. The other is similarly baffled by "Blu-ray."

3. One of you doesn't own a checkbook, and wouldn't know how to write a check. The other can't figure out how to bank on line, and doesn't want to learn.

4. One of you wears a watch. The other looks at his/her phone.

5.. One of you orders a half-caff, double-shot skim macchiato. The other prefers coffee.

6. One of you thinks Woodward and Bernstein is a law firm. The other thinks Android is a movie about aliens.

Final words of caution:

Before bridging the generation gap, you should know many younger men think killing spiders is equal opportunity employment, while an older man might expect you to butter his toast. And then there's that heart-stopping moment when you see a picture of his mother (or daughter) and realize you went to school with her.

CHAPTER 4

ONLINE DATING

So where do you find a suitable husband? In the days when couples got married in their 20s, it was easier. You could shop in your English Poetry class. Or, if you wanted someone a little more down to earth, you could hang around the Electrical Engineering building. But today most women don't start thinking about marriage until they're in their 30s, and the opportunity to shop in a concentrated environment is long gone. And what about the widows, divorcées and single moms? Where do they go?

It would be great if you could go to the supermarket and say, "I'll take a melon, a dozen eggs and the cute guy in the green sweater on Aisle Six." Unfortunately, it doesn't work that way.

No, today, just as you shop online for music, books, prescription drugs and (my personal recommendation) support hose, you'll probably have to go online to find a suitable husband. (I'm told it's also a very discrete way to purchase adult diapers, should the need arise.)

Being married more than 50 years ago, I'm more familiar with Amazon and eBay than I am with dating sites. So the following is based strictly on secondary research.

The first thing I learned is that there are a lot of choices. Beyond Match.com, Tinder and eHarmony, there are sites like Badoo, where you can meet people in your area to chat, date or start a casual friendship; RightStuff, a dating site for Ivy Leaguers; Tastebuds.fm, which matches people up based on their music preferences. Then there are BeautifulPeople.com and MensaMatch.com, should you feel qualified.

For older daters there's OurTime; SinglesOver60; SinglesOver70, and SeniorBlackPeopleMeet.

Cheaters might want to check out AdultFriendFinder and Gleeden, which are similar to the infamously-hacked AshleyMadison.com. Of course, there's always the grim possibility you'll wind up on the front page of your hometown newspaper.

Even more specialized are EquestrianSingles. com, Geek2Geek, Democratic PeopleMeet as well as RepublicanPeopleMeet, MustLovePets, FarmersOnly, TrekPassions (as in Trekkies; a good place to find a nerd – see Chapter 2), VeggieDate.org, etc.

Take your pick. There's apparently no reason for anyone to sit home on a Saturday night.

Once you've decided on one or more sites, the next step is to write a compelling profile. Natalia Lusinski, who writes dating profiles for eCyrano.com, says to avoid clichés: "I like candlelit dinners, sunsets and walks on the beach." Who doesn't? On the other hand: "My most memorable experiences were climbing Kilimanjaro, seeing the sun rise over the Grand Canyon and placing a bet at the casino in Monte Carlo" will get you attention.

But the most important part of the profile is your picture. You want something that reveals who you are but not too much. (Kim Kardashian is an object lesson.) And no corporate headshots. He's looking for a date, not a new CFO.

If you're tempted to submit a photo that was taken 20 pounds and two double-chins ago, be sure there aren't any give-aways in the background – like a rotary phone or typewriter.

When evaluating responses, online daters tell me that men generally lie. They're always two inches shorter, five years older and one tax bracket less successful. A "transportation manager" may turn out to be an Uber driver. Proceed with caution.

One dating-site veteran says, "I've got a pretty good built-in b.s. detector when it comes to sizing up people on the Internet. For instance, a guy can tell me he's got a Ph.D., but if his grammar, spelling and syntax are poor, I know he's lying. If he presents himself as a wealthy, sophisticated person, I'll ask him about his travels: where he's been, where he's stayed, what he saw, etc. Any idiot can say he owns a Mercedes-Benz, but if someone describes his travels to me, I believe him. I've been right more times than not."

Then there's Carol, who corresponded online with a man who said he was a lawyer, was tall, liked to walk on the beach and loved to travel. They agreed to meet at a restaurant. She got there early and found a seat by the window so she could watch for her mystery date. When she didn't see anyone who remotely looked like the person she was waiting for, she left.

When she got home there was a message from him, stating that he was at the restaurant and didn't see her. They agreed to meet again, this time for drinks. As she was waiting, an older man, old enough to be her father, rolled up in a wheelchair.

"I thought to myself, 'Six feet tall? Likes to walk on the beach? Loves to travel? Maybe he should update his profile.'"

First dates should be in public places. Starbucks is made for this. And be sure to establish an exit strategy before meeting. "I have a [sick dog, dinner plans, papers to grade], but I'd love to get together for a half hour."

Have your antennae out. Beware the warning signs! As anyone with a telephone or an email address knows, there are a lot of scammers out there. Here are some tip-offs:

- He "falls in love" with you too quickly.

- He wants you to remove your dating profile.

- He talks about trips you can take next year.

- He's vague about where he works, what he does, where he lives.

- He has a sob story or a "great investment opportunity." (Either should set off sirens, sending you to the nearest emergency exit.)

That said, there are lots of cyber success stories. (My son and daughter-in-law met online.) But there are just as many mismatches, weirdos and flat-out con artists. Shoppers, beware.

CHAPTER 5

LIGHTLY USED MERCHANDISE

You may have wanted a brand, spanking-new husband, but the one you got had a previous owner. Everything is fine under the hood, the motor purrs like a kitten, but he's got a few miles on the tires and a scratch or two on the left rear bumper.

Selecting a pre-owned husband has its pros and cons. On the one hand he's already broken in. Someone else taught him to put down the toilet seat, bring you tea and honey when you're sick and tell you your butt looks fine.

On the other hand, used husbands often come with a few encumbrances like a random child or two and at least one deranged ex-wife. (By definition, they're always deranged.)

If you have a choice, find a man who has sons rather than daughters. They'll either ignore you or accept you, but they won't engage you in mortal combat over Daddy's affection.

All stepchildren are tricky, however. Unlike newborn babies, they have pre-existing expectations, behavior patterns, likes and dislikes. You have to adapt to them; they will not, under any circumstances, adapt to you. And even though you may be paying for half their tuition and braces, you don't get to select the school or the orthodontist.

The younger the children, the more issues will arise. But if you bide your time and play the long game, you can look forward to a rewarding relationship in the future – like when they're middle-aged and have to decide whether or not to put you in a home.

Even without children, being a second wife has its challenges. In addition to the ex-wife, there are ex-in-laws, friends, neighbors and co-workers who knew and perhaps even liked the first wife. (I'm sure even Lizzie Borden had friends.) Unless you create a new circle of friends, you'll run the risk of always coming in second.

You will, however, have one major advantage a first wife can never claim. Your battle-scarred husband selected you when he was more mature and had a better understanding of what he wanted from a relationship. Furthermore, he was willing to take a chance on marriage knowing how painful its dissolution can be. As Oscar Wilde once said: "Second marriages – the triumph of hope over experience."

He has to really love you to risk it all again. And who doesn't want that?

CHAPTER 6

ALTERNATIVE STRATEGY

The primary reason it's so hard to stay married is that men and women are inherently different. We've been told we're from two different planets – Venus vs. Mars – right? Men are hunters. Women are gatherers. OK, we get it. We're genetically unsuited to live with each other.

That's why I strongly favor same-sex marriages . . . even for people who aren't gay. Just imagine, you and your partner would like the same movies, read the same books. You might even talk about them.

Plus you'd have a live-in wardrobe consultant. If I ask Jack Schindler what he thinks of my outfit, he always says the same thing: "I don't see anything wrong with it."

Well, thank you very much. I feel so much more confident now.

But if I asked another woman, I'd get a constructive answer. Perhaps she'd say, "I think the blue is better with your eyes." Or she might say, "It makes you look 10 pounds thinner." Or she could even add, "What shoes will you wear?" Good question!

Now I ask you: Is there a man on the face of the earth who would inquire about

your accessories? Not one who's straight.

This isn't just my opinion. Studies have shown that same-sex couples actually are more compatible than heterosexual couples. Not so surprisingly, they have better communication, fewer conflicts and a more equitable division of labor. Sounds pretty good, doesn't it?

Of course, I admit, there's the pesky issue of sex. But stop and ask yourself: How much of my life is spent having sex and how much of is spent doing other things – like unloading the dishwasher? Can you honestly say you have sex more often than you unload the dishwasher?*

Think it over. You don't have to commit right now.

But for those of you who are still interested in the opposite sex, let's go back to the manual and the issue of "Buyer's Remorse."

* This test is not applicable to 20-year-olds who don't own dishwashers.

CHAPTER 7

YOU GET WHAT YOU GET

Never marry a man thinking you can change him. It's not possible. They are pre-programmed at the factory and the settings can't be changed.

Don't expect him to learn to dance, eat Indian food, dress better, stop drinking, improve his grammar, spend less money or spend more money. If he didn't do it before marriage, he isn't going to do it later.

Face it: eating in his underwear, leaving crumbs on the counter and taking the sports pages into the bathroom are his default settings. Get used to it.

It's far better to take a hard look at a man and decide what you can live with and what you can't before marriage. What are your deal breakers? I've created this chart to help us evaluate and rank some less desirable male qualities.

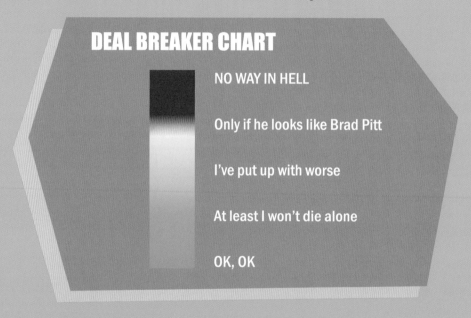

DEAL BREAKER CHART

NO WAY IN HELL

Only if he looks like Brad Pitt

I've put up with worse

At least I won't die alone

OK, OK

As you can see it ranges from a decided NO WAY IN HELL – to a submissive OK, OK. So here are my personal rankings.

Physical abuse?	*That'd be way up on top.*
Drug or alcohol abuse?	*Probably not.*

Gambling, cheating?	*I might be able to live with it.*
Bad dresser?	*How bad?*
Can't dance?	*Disappointing – but not critical.*
Farts in bed?	*Well, they all do that.*

Now let's review your deal breakers. What turns you off?

How do you feel about men who speak to you in a condescending "man-voice"? You know the one: "OK, Amy, if that's what you think, far be it from me to correct you."

Where would that rank for you?

What about: Falls asleep one minute after sex?

How would you feel if he went drinking with his co-workers every night instead of coming home?

Or, how about: He has dinner with his mother once a week, and you're not invited?

Here's another issue: What if you caught a boyfriend trying on your pantyhose? When it happened to my friend Nicole, she headed for the door. On the other hand, Kris Jenner bought XXL pantyhose and went on with her life for 14 years.

(She only left when her husband Bruce/Caitlyn started to look as good in a cocktail dress as she did.)

What if you were a gorgeous, celebrated TV personality, a member of America's most famous political family, and you found out your muscle-bound governor husband had a secret love child?

We know what Maria Shriver did.

Customer Service Call

Judi: *Technical Support, may I help you?*

Caller: *I have a problem with my husband.*

Judi: *Well, of course you do.*

Caller: *Every time he drives the car, he goes berserk. If another driver is too slow or misses a left-turn arrow, he screams, bangs on the steering wheel and honks. And if, God forbid, anyone should cut him off...*

Judi: *How long has this been going on?*

Caller: *Ten years.*

Judi: *How long have you been married?*

Caller: *Ten years. What should I do?*

Judi: *Turn up the radio.*

CHAPTER 8

TOGETHERNESS AND OTHER MYTHS

I've spent most of my married life trying to find something my husband and I can do together. I ski. He doesn't. He watches sports. I don't. I ride a bike. He never learned. I love theater. He prefers wrestling matches. We don't enjoy the same television programs, books or movies. (The Multiplex has been a Godsend. We can each see the film of our choice and meet up afterwards for dinner.)

Dr. Phil says that the notion that a great relationship requires common interests is a myth. He says, "If you and your partner are forcing yourselves to engage in common activities but the results are stress, tension and conflict, don't do it."

I wish I had consulted with Dr. Phil before I made the decision, a few years ago, that Jack and I should take up golf. Neither of us played, so I thought it would be perfect. We'd learn together. We'd join a country club. We'd travel to golf resorts around the world. I could see us putting off into the sunset in our golden years.

So we each bought clubs and took a series of lessons. We even went on an intensive golf-school weekend. Turns out, I have no hand-eye coordination. Golf would always be an exercise in futility and humiliation for me. And, truth be told, he had no intention of playing golf with me. He only wanted to be able to take part in golf outings with the guys.

I gave away my clubs. His were stolen. (At least that's what he told me.)

When I recovered from my disappointment, I told him it was his turn to come up with a suggestion.

"What do you think we could do together?" I asked. He thought about it a while and then brightened and said, "How about duck hunting?"

I said, "You want me to get up at 4 in the morning, put on waders, hide in a duck blind and shoot Donald and Daffy?"

Dr. Phil is right.

CHAPTER 9

THE CARE AND FEEDING OF THE MALE EGO

Here's a fact of life that I accept, although it goes against my feminist grain: No matter how old a woman is, she still wants to be attractive to men.

My mother, Rosalie, who died at 98 years of age, had two boyfriends toward the end. John was visually impaired, but he went to the drugstore with her and helped her get her walker out of the car. Bill brought her flowers on her birthdays and accompanied her to a wedding. They fought over who was going to take her to the beauty shop. I'm convinced that Bill and John added 10 years to her life.

Mom told me that having two men find her attractive gave her a reason to get out of bed in the morning. Even one would have been nice.

While women want to be attractive, men want something different. No matter how old they get, they want to be admired and looked up to (even when they're sitting in a wheelchair).

They want us to think they're smarter, stronger and braver than we are. Let them think we do.

My theory is that when men leave their wives, it's not because they find someone better, but because they find someone who admires them more than their wives do. However, it's a lot easier to admire a man if you've never washed his underwear.

The tabloids are filled with stories about famous men who trade in their old wives for newer, glossier versions. Brad Pitt comes to mind, and look how well that turned out. Rupert Murdoch has married four times. There have been five Mrs. Billy Bob Thorntons. And Larry King has walked down the aisle a total of eight times. My guess? They're just looking for a more appreciative audience.

I'm not going to tell you to let him beat you in tennis or to swoon at his manly strength when he opens a jar of pickles. But just like cars need an occasional tune-up, husbands need an occasional ego boost.

Here are some suggestions:

- Brag about him in front of friends: "Roger has a great sense of direction. He never makes a wrong turn."
- Appeal to his vanity: "Did you really go to school with those guys? You look so much younger."
- And most important, overlook his failings: "Nobody could have done it better."

Protecting a man's ego is fundamental to maintaining a long-term marriage.

CHAPTER 10

CRACKING THE CODE

It's time to acknowledge that men and women are not only different; they speak different languages. Relationship expert Julie-Ann Shapiro says that men speak "Menglish," which sounds exactly the same as normal English, but words and phrases can have entirely different meanings.

For this reason, you sometimes need a translator when speaking to a husband. Here are a few simple phrases you should commit to memory.

"I'll do it later" means, "I'll never do it."

"I'll think about it" means, "Think about what?"

"There's nothing for me to eat." This phrase has many different interpretations. In some homes, it means, "Who ate my potato chips?" Or, "Where are the pretzels?" Or, "Why don't we have a whole roasted chicken and a ham in our house at all times?" In my house, it usually means, we're out of cheese. It almost never means you're out of kale.

"I joined a bowling league" means, "I never wanted to have a third child."

"I need time to find myself" means, "I have a girlfriend."

"We're growing in different directions" means, "I have a girlfriend who's 10 years younger than you."

"I'm just not happy" means, "I have a pregnant girlfriend who's 10 years younger than you." So you can see why he's not happy.

CHAPTER 11

COMMUNICATION STRATEGIES

Let us now discuss that all-important question: communication.

I always say that the secret of my marriage is that in 50+ years, my husband and I have never had a single, meaningful conversation.

We try to keep our discussions to "Honey, did you replace the toilet paper?" "We're out of ice." And "I have a rash on my elbow."

Want to pour your heart out? Call a girlfriend. I know a young woman who broke up with her boyfriend because he never talked to her. Of course he didn't.

It's a scientific fact that the reason men and women have communication problems is that our brains operate differently. According to Gregory L. Jantz, Ph.D., writing in *Psychology Today*, scientists have discovered approximately 100 gender differences between the male brain and the female brain. Male brains tend to focus narrowly on one task or concept at a time, while female brains process and connect a wide variety of data and can absorb more sensory information.

This explains what happens when a man and woman sit down together in a restaurant. She's thinking about the decor, the air conditioning, the people sitting around her, the waiter's uniform, whether her skirt's too short and whether the woman who just walked in is someone she knew in high school.

He's thinking, "Steak."

Here is a tidbit from Dr. Jantz that will surprise no one: Females have verbal centers on both sides of the brain, while males have verbal centers only on the left hemisphere. Men not only have fewer verbal centers, they also have less connectivity between their word center and their memories or feelings – so much for discussing their emotions.

This is why you should never try to talk about feelings with a man. It will not end well. Trust me.

I once broke this rule. It was our 25th or 30th anniversary, and I wanted to find out what my husband liked about me. I know he loves me, but why? I was hoping to hear it was because I am pretty or smart or funny – or because I make his life an adventure. Did I get the answer I was looking for? No, my husband said that the thing he likes best about me is that I'm his.

I realize some people think that is sweet, but I know the truth. He doesn't have a clue. All he knows is, I am the one he wakes up with every morning, and he's not that crazy about change.

Customer Service Call

Judi: Technical Support. How may I help you?

Caller: I have a problem with my boyfriend.

Judi: I'm here for you.

Caller: We're both in our early 30s, and we've been dating for five years. We're very happy in every way, but I can't get him to talk about marriage. He just walks out of the room.

Judi: That's because you're asking him to discuss the end of all life on this planet, as he knows it. You need to break it down into smaller bits. Has he ever said he doesn't want to get married?

Caller: No.

Judi: Good. Then it's just a matter of details. Give him one or two simple choices. No essay questions. One day you ask, "Do you prefer spring weddings or fall?" Then another day, you might say, "I think I'd like just family to attend, or would you want to include friends?" Before you know it, you'll be walking down the aisle.

Caller: Thanks.

Judi: Let me know how it goes.

Now that the subject of proposals has come up, I have a confession to make. Jack Schindler never asked me to marry him. When we first started dating, I told him I didn't want to get married. And every so often I would remind him that I was committed to being single for the rest of my life.

Then one day, after about a year, I told him I'd changed my mind. He was relieved, and I was engaged.

CHAPTER 12

NO UNSOLICITED ADVICE

What do I mean, "no unsolicited advice"?

Yes, yes, you're right. We're all so wise. We know exactly how everyone else should live his life. Just do precisely what we tell you to do.

But face it: Nobody likes unsolicited advice, particularly men, particularly men who are married to an advice-giver. I'm not sure they like advice even when they ask for it.

If my husband turns to me in the car and asks, "Should we take Lake Shore Drive or the expressway?" he's not asking for advice. He just wants to be able to blame me if we wind up in a traffic jam.

Let's face it, unsolicited advice is often an implied criticism. For example when you say: "You should get a haircut," aren't you actually saying, "Your hair's too long"?

A harmless suggestion like, "You should read this book," can sound like, "You should pick up a book once in a while. There's more to life than ESPN."

And don't think you can disguise unsolicited advice in the form of a question.

"You're going to eat all that?" has only one possible interpretation: "You're a fat pig."

"Are you going to shower before we go out for dinner?" clearly means, "You're a filthy pig." (Unless there's an issue with your hot water heater. In that case, never mind.)

Unsolicited advice can't be disguised in the form of a gift, either. You may want to rethink tucking a nose-hair trimmer into his Christmas stocking or that gift certificate for back waxing.

Even concerned advice like, "Try taking an aspirin for your headache." Or, "Why don't you order the fish?" sounds, God forbid, like you're telling him what to do. Some men, particularly the one I've been acquainted with for 50 years or more, will do exactly the opposite just to show who's boss.

Of course, you never, ever make a suggestion about his work, even if he complains about his boss every night for a week. While it may seem like he's asking for advice, he's not. He only wants to vent in the vicinity of a sympathetic, warm body. Your job is to be that body.

I have a technique you might like to try. Just nod your head, and say, "Is that so?" You might even click your tongue as you nod. I suggest practicing this technique every day. It also works well with adolescent children, aging parents and friends who complain about *their* husbands.

CHAPTER 13

ACCESSORIES AND UPGRADES

Does this happen to you? Every time you get a new phone, computer or software program, your entire life turns upside down.

Nothing works the way you think it should. You have to learn all new procedures. You push one button, and the wrong window opens. You push another, and the whole thing crashes.

Then you spend hours on the phone with some guy on a help desk in India, who pretends his name is Jason. In the long run, you're happy with the upgrade, but it takes a while to get there.

That's kind of like adding children to a marriage, or I should say *relationship*, because I realize that many couples today have reversed the order.

In any case, children change everything – your daily routine, division of labor, sleeping habits, sex drive, cash flow, insurance needs, free time, body, laundry loads per week, the car you drive, grocery bills, social life, where you live and how long it takes to get out the door. Not to mention your priorities.

You used to have a perfect living room – *House Beautiful* down to the last throw pillow. Now there are toys, strollers and wet diapers wherever you look.

That's a life-altering adjustment. I firmly believe babies start out small and helpless so you can get used to them a little at a time. They literally grow on you. Can you imagine if they came out as full-blown, smart-mouthed teenagers? You couldn't build enough orphanages.

My husband and I were married more than eight years before our son was born. So we had an established, well-grounded relationship before adding another human being to the mix. I suspect that procreating before marriage is a lot tougher even when couples have lived together for a while.

Although Jack and I were more mature than the day we married, we still didn't know the first thing about raising a child.

Frankly, I would argue that no one knows anything about raising children. That's why they keep rewriting the rulebook. The one I read advocated pre-made formula, baby food in jars, playpens, cribs, bumpers on cribs and letting baby cry himself to sleep. We never heard of swaddling, and if we knew someone slept with their infant, we'd call child protective services.

It's amazing anyone born before the millennium survived.

Jack and I were particularly clueless. When our son was a baby, he developed a rash on his penis. My husband, who believes Neosporin can cure anything, slathered the baby's penis with the anti-bacterial. Then, to make sure the ointment wouldn't rub off, he covered it with a Band-Aid.

No, that is not a misprint. He actually taped a Band-Aid to the baby's penis!

You've never heard such screaming. And guess who had to call the pediatrician and ask, "Dr. Rice, how do you get a Band-Aid off a penis?"

The answer was, "soak him in a warm tub." You might write that down, in case you ever face the same dilemma. On second thought, I doubt you will.

CHAPTER 14

IN AND OUTLAWS

The first step to building a great relationship with your husband's parents is to figure out what to call them. I know it's awkward calling people you may have just met "Mom and Dad," but you have to call them something – and the sooner the better. "Harold and Hortense?" "Mr. and Mrs. Gobsocker?" "Mother and Father Gobsocker?" Ask them what they prefer, but for God's sake, call them something.

Many the timid bride has prayed her mother-in-law would look in her direction so she could start a conversation or tell her that her hair's on fire. Real cowards hold off until their first child is born so they can start calling them "Grandma and Grandpa." (With a little luck, no one will experience spontaneous combustion before that.)

Speaking of children, don't be surprised if they change the entire dynamic of your relationship with you in-laws. You're likely to see them more often and receive a lot more unsolicited advice. (See Chapter 12.)

And be prepared: You may have to set boundaries on gift-giving, candy, cartoon programs, curse words, car seats and (if you live in Texas) loaded handguns.

When I was first married, my late, much-loved mother-in-law thought everything I did was wonderful. I had total approval for the way I dressed, entertained, ran a home and treated her son. Then I had a child.

After that, nothing I did was right. It was either "too windy to go out" or "fresh air would be good for the baby." His hat was ether too tight or too loose. And his food was either too hot or too cold.

Finally one day, I told my mother-in-law it hurt my feelings that she didn't have confidence in my ability to be a mother. She never said another word.

It's in your best interest to maintain a good relationship with your in-laws, particularly when there are children. They're usually eager babysitters, and you'll secure your place in their will.

But sometimes you just can't.

Brittany Wong of *The Huffington Post* writes about one MIL who told her DIL such things as, "Nancy, it's not that you're fat, you're just short." "I like you better than [her other daughter-in-law] Kathleen; you don't have a big nose." And "Nancy, does Bobby hate me? You know I didn't want him."

What if your in-laws are really awful – straight out of a Dickens or Stephen King novel? The MIL is a manipulative, possessive harridan who talks about you behind your back. And the FIL is an overbearing racist who keeps snakes as a hobby. In that case, forget good relationships. Go for self-preservation.

Here's a tip. Visit the website www.ihatemyinlaws.com, and read about other people's in-law grievances. You can use the site to vent your own frustrations or just take comfort in the fact that you're not alone.

If all else fails, screw the will and put as much distance between yourself and the in-laws as possible, up to and including a move to Saskatchewan.

Customer Service Call

Judi: *Technical Support. May I help you?*

Caller: *I have a problem with my husband.*

Judi: *Why am I not surprised?*

Caller: *He's a total mama's boy. She calls him several times a week, and he goes running. Sometimes it's to fix a leaky faucet or mow her lawn. One time she called to have him change a light bulb. Any advice?*

Judi: *Next time marry an orphan.*

CHAPTER 15

HOW TO REBOOT

You know how when your computer starts slowing down or won't open certain programs, you just click on "restart"? Or when your TV is misbehaving, you unplug it, plug it back in and suddenly it's fixed? Well there's a way to reboot a husband who's grumpy or uncommunicative.

All you have to do is... *wait for it*... initiate sex.

Don't be coy or shy about it. Candlelight and plunging neckline might not be enough. If he's really grumpy, you may have to be a little more direct.

Here's a suggestion: Call him up at work one day and say, "You know, I've been thinking about your penis all day." Crazy as it sounds, he'll actually believe you.

If that's not your style, try one of these:

- Put a note in his briefcase or lunch bucket telling him you'll be wearing a black lace bra and garters when he gets home that night.

- Send him a text message with a photo of you in above-mentioned lace bra and garters.

- When you're out in public, whisper to him that you aren't wearing any underwear.

- Take him on a shopping trip to a sex-toy store.

- Offer to give him a full body massage, with special emphasis on the full body.

It's simple. Try it. You're welcome.

CHAPTER 16

THE ROOT OF ALL EVIL

In the 50+ years I've been married to Jack Schindler, we've fought about whether the windows should be open or the windows should be closed, whether the lights should be on or off, whether it's too hot or too cold, whether to stay home or go out and what time we have to leave for the airport. We argue about food, television, politics, clothing, landscaping, interior design and whether to turn right or left.

The only thing we've never fought about is money. And the reason we don't fight about money is that we maintain separate bank accounts and credit cards.

All accounts are in both names, but I never look at his statements, and he never looks at mine. Over the years, we just divvied up who pays for what without ever discussing it.

I used to do all the grocery shopping, so I paid for groceries. Twenty-five years ago, he took over the shopping, but I still give him a check to pay for it.

At one point early in our marriage, we decided that we should live off his income and bank mine. The first week, I told him I would need some money for groceries.

"I'll see if I can give you something at the end of the month," he said.

Believing, as I did, that one of us might get hungry before the end of the month, I called an end to the experiment. We seemed to have fundamental differences when it came to financial priorities. So we just went back to the old system of separate income and expenditures and never discussed it again.

The truth: When one partner holds the purse strings, there's an imbalance of power, which is not healthy.

In my opinion, even women without an independent income deserve financial autonomy.

Customer Service Call

Judi: *Technical Support. How may I help you?*

Caller: *I have a problem with my husband.*

Judi: *Big surprise!*

Caller: *When he retired, he decided I didn't need a credit card or a checkbook anymore because he goes everywhere with me.*

Judi: *That's a scary thought.*

Caller: *If we go to the grocery store, he pays the bill. If I shop for clothes or household goods, he oversees what I buy. If I go to the hair salon, he doles out some cash. What should I do? Frankly, I've been thinking about divorce.*

Judi: *Divorce, no. Put your foot down. Either he goes back to work or you do. Someone has to get out of that house.*

These days, the pendulum can swing the other way, which is another reason you might want separate accounts. I heard of a young woman who financed a car for her boyfriend because he was unable to get credit. When they moved in together, they opened a joint checking account, which he frequently overdrew. Finally, she told him she was taking his name off the account. An hour later, he broke up with her.

CHAPTER 17

THE GIFT OF GIFT-GIVING

When we first get married, we think, "If my husband really loved me, he'd know exactly what I want for my birthday [or our anniversary, giving birth, Mother's Day, Valentine's Day, Arbor Day, etc.]."

No, he would not. Get that notion out of your head immediately, Young Lady.

Gift-giving is a skill with which most men are not factory equipped. They need some not-so-subtle coaching. First, you must teach him that acknowledging you with a gift will not emasculate him. And, second, it's not the thought that counts.

The right gift is one that's useful, but not too useful – maybe a little luxurious. It should reflect your taste, not his. And it shouldn't be a disguised criticism. In other words, vacuum cleaners, beer coolers and Thigh Masters: bad gifts.

Jewelry, on the other hand, is always in good taste. But I'm sure you knew that already.

Here are a few different training methods you might employ:

- **Lead by Example:** When your birthday is coming up, you can say to your husband, "Did you see the necklace Todd gave Lana? It's stunning. She'll treasure it forever and pass it down to their daughters." You don't have to add, "unlike the Dustbuster you gave me last year."

- **Enlist a Double Agent:** Another technique is to recruit a trusted friend (preferably female – sister, daughter, mother, neighbor) to ask him what he's going to get you for your anniversary, Mother's Day, etc. If he lacks a good answer, she can offer a suggestion (thoughtfully provided by you) and, if necessary, go shopping with him.

- **Skip Subtle:** If all else fails, you can flat-out tell him. I know that might take the fun out of it, but you'll get what you want, and he'll be grateful to opt out of the guessing game.

- **A word of caution:** Never return a husband's gift. A friend of mine got a brooch for her first anniversary, which she exchanged for an even lovelier bracelet that was more to her taste. Fifty years later, she's never received another piece of jewelry from her husband. Lesson learned.

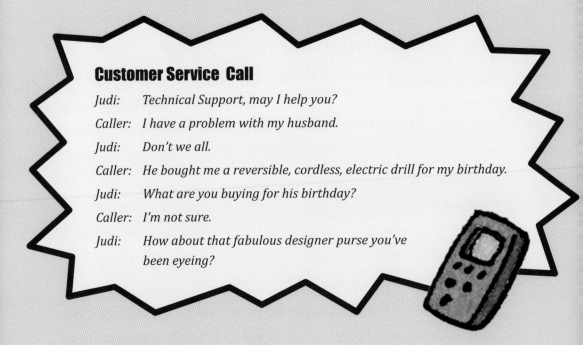

Customer Service Call

Judi: *Technical Support, may I help you?*

Caller: *I have a problem with my husband.*

Judi: *Don't we all.*

Caller: *He bought me a reversible, cordless, electric drill for my birthday.*

Judi: *What are you buying for his birthday?*

Caller: *I'm not sure.*

Judi: *How about that fabulous designer purse you've been eyeing?*

CHAPTER 18

TOILET TRAINING

By now you know I'm an easy-going kinda gal. I believe you get what you get, you put up with a lot of petty annoyances and you don't ask for meaningful conversations. But here's where I draw the line.

The toilet seat must go down. No debate. No compromise. And you must insist from the start. Otherwise one day, when you're a little older and can no longer sleep through the night, you'll get up, go to the bathroom with your eyes still closed and... fall in.

A pretty rude surprise at 2 a.m., I can tell you. (Now that I think about it, here's another reason in favor of same-sex marriages. Just add it to the list.)

I recently saw a sign posted over the toilet in someone's home. It read:

"Notice: The last man who forgot to put the toilet seat down is buried in the backyard."

I'm not sure how effective this would be, but feel free to give it a try. (The signage, not the burial.)

You're not going to believe the following, but I saw it on the internet so it must be true.

A researcher at Michigan State University by the name of Jay Pil Choe has done a thorough economic analysis of toilet-seat etiquette. He based his study on the premise that men stand up to pee and sit down to poop, while women sit for both functions. Therefore, if you leave the seat up, men are occasionally inconvenienced and women are always inconvenienced. If you put it down, only men have to change the seat position. and only sometimes.

His formula, which I won't pretend to understand, concludes that toilet-seat equity is based on the number of males to females living in the same home.

Essentially, if the ratio of men to women in the household is equal, the toilet seat should stay down. On the other hand, if there are four males in the household, the toilet seat stays up when there are two or fewer women.

I bring up this study, which can be found online at https://www.msu.edu/~choijay/etiquette.pdf, only in the interest of providing you with a more rational argument than, "If you really loved me, you'd put the seat down."

Ladies, we have to stick together on this one. We don't expect them to pull out our chairs anymore, or tip their baseball caps or walk on the street side of the sidewalk. But we must fight to the last woman to maintain this final vestige of chivalry.

CHAPTER 19

RETURN POLICY

There may come a day when you look at your husband and think, "Where's that thoughtful, affectionate guy who waited for me at the altar and promised to love and cherish me for better or worse, in sickness and health? This bozo has some flaws that weren't listed on the label."

So what can you do?

Can you claim fraud, ship him back to the manufacturer and ask for a refund? Can you drive him to the Used Husband Lot and trade him in for a newer model? Can you donate him to Goodwill and take a tax deduction?

You can try, but chances are you're going to have to file for divorce, which is expensive, messy, demoralizing and likely to screw up your plans for the holidays.

While I don't speak from experience, I know enough divorce lawyers to know that once they're brought into the picture, the process of uncoupling becomes immediately adversarial, and the longer the negotiations go on, the bigger the fee. Your lawyer's job is to get you the best possible deal. And your husband's lawyer has the very same job description.

By definition, someone has to win, and someone has to lose. (Or both parties lose while the lawyers make a killing.)

The late Robin Williams once said, "Ah yes, divorce, from the Latin word meaning, 'to rip out a man's genitals through his wallet.'" And with women so often the breadwinner, it can also mean ripping out her heart and her self-esteem through her IRA.

According to the legal website www.nolo.com, the average uncontested divorce costs $14,500.

Divorces that go to trial average $19,600. And, of course, the more money involved, the more there is to fight over and the more it's going to cost.

Unless there are complicated tax or financial issues, most couples are probably better off coming to a basic agreement between themselves before bringing in the hired guns. Mediators can also bring the cost down. And young couples without a great deal of assets, might be able to file the paperwork themselves.

Even if you inadvertently married an insufferable, lying, cheating, drunken brute (and I'm sure you did), you're better off ending the divorce as amicably as possible. It's not only cheaper, but chances are this is not the last you are going to see of this guy.

Face it: If children are involved, there's really no such thing as a divorce. You can divide your net worth, live in different homes and file separate tax returns, but you are inextricably bound to each other for life. It starts with joint custody and child support issues and continues through every parent-teacher conference, vacation schedule, graduation, wedding and funeral plus some awkward holidays with his hateful new wife thrown in for good measure.

And speaking of his hateful new wife, she's going to want a say on whether little Whitney can get parts of her anatomy pierced or tattooed or whether teen-age Jordan should be given his own car. Every disagreement will find you on the wrong side of two against one.

This what they really mean by "'Til death do you part."

CHAPTER 20

BUT NOT FOR LUNCH

You know the joke: "I married him for better or worse, but not for lunch."

It's no joke.

Note to newlyweds: DO NOT SKIP THIS CHAPTER.
It is essential reading as preparation for a long-term marriage.

I hereby go on record as saying that no human being should suffer the agony of unremitting togetherness.

When one or both of you retire, you must fight hard to preserve your independence. Continue pursuing your own interests, friends and activities. Then when you do get together, hopefully no more than once or twice a week, you'll have something interesting to talk about.

Someone once told me that having your husband retire means half the income and twice the husband. I didn't know exactly what she meant until my husband and I both retired and I was suddenly placed under 24-hour surveillance.

Even if you didn't work outside the home before retirement, chances are you managed to fill those hours between nine to five quite nicely, thank you. You may have run the house, hauled the kids around, volunteered, pursued hobbies, paid taxes, served on non-profit boards, arranged flowers, practiced belly dancing or read an occasional book.

At this late stage, you certainly don't need anyone to monitor your phone calls or critique the way you stock the pantry or chop an onion. And you certainly don't need someone to accompany you on a shopping trip if that someone has no patience for shopping and can't tell whether a new outfit makes you look fat.

I was still working when my husband retired. I felt bad for him, because he didn't seem to be doing much. The highlight of his day was a walk to Starbuck's for coffee, and he doesn't even like coffee. So one day I invited him to attend a workshop where I was one of the speakers.

Everything was going fine, until I looked over at him from the podium and saw that he was mouthing instructions to me. I had no idea what he was trying to say, so I was forced to interrupt my presentation and announce, "Ladies and gentlemen, I believe my husband has something to add to the topic."

Turns out, he wanted to remind me to distribute a hand-out I'd brought. Apparently, he felt strongly enough about the issue to stop the show. (Who says he has control issues?)

When Jack first talked about retirement, I asked him what he wanted to do with all that free time. He looked at me, and – with a straight face – said he wanted to buy a camper so the two of us could drive around the country together.

He saw us tooling down the open road with no particular destination, free as birds, with our passports in the glove compartment in case we wanted to pop over to Mexico or Canada where our medications are cheaper.

I saw us trapped in a tin can on wheels, preparing meals in a microwave oven and bickering every moment over which road to take and when to stop for a bathroom break.

When all is said and done, I'd rather go duck hunting.

CHAPTER 21

TRADE-INS

(Note to newlyweds: Bookmark this chapter and come back to it in 10 years.)

So if divorce has its drawbacks, and murder is messy, what other options do you have when you need to take a break from the bonds of holy matrimony?

After all, 50 years is a long time to stay married to anybody. Even Rosalynn Carter must have days when she'd like to send Jimmy back to the peanut farm.

We don't stick with the same shade of lipstick for a lifetime. Sometime we want a change of pace – "siren red" rather than "bashful blush" – to see how it feels. (I'm not talking about divorce, just a new face on the pillow for little while.)

I think you should be able to swap out husbands for short periods of time – a little vacation, some R&R, a change of scene.

Maybe you'd part with the one who has good manners for a sleeker model who's a great dancer. Or, if the one who cracks his knuckles is driving you crazy, maybe you want to sample the one who just leaves crumbs on the kitchen counter or drops his wet towel on the bathroom floor.

You know those websites, "Vacation Rentals by Owner (VRBO.com) or

HomeExchange.com, where homeowners can rent out their residences or swap with other homeowners?

I'm thinking of starting a similar website, which would be called something like "Hubby Rental by Owner," or "He-Bay." Maybe even "Pop Swap."

Wives could place an ad and see what offers they get.

If Annette Bening wanted to trade in Warren Beatty, her ad might read: "Legendary heartbreaker and inspiration for Carly Simon's 'You're So Vain' now fully house-trained and domesticated. Price recently reduced."

And surely Beyoncé could stand a break from JAY-Z's rumored infidelities. Her ad might read: "Aging rapper billionaire. Comes with extensive wardrobe. Has learned to play nice with in-laws. Will trade for anyone."

And, finally, here's the ad I might place: "Gently used, 78-year-old, retired insurance executive. Still has hair and teeth. Newly installed knee. Drives at night. All offers will be considered."

Any takers? Shoot me a text message.

CHAPTER 22

REPLACEMENT PARTS & WARRANTIES

Here's some good news. You may not be able to get replacement parts for your old vacuum cleaner, but you can get them for your husband. He can get fixed up with a new knee, a new hip or hair plugs – just like that. And if another part of the anatomy goes on the fritz, there are those little blue pills or even implants. I'm told that the implants work with the touch of a button – much better than the original equipment.

Other body parts, however, don't remain in like-new condition. They quickly lose that new car smell.

After about 20 years of marriage, husbands begin suffering from "wife deafness." (This phenomenon has no relationship to "nose blindness," which is characterized by the inability to recognize that your home smells like sweat socks or cat urine.)

I was at a dinner party recently with four other long-married couples. Every woman had the same complaint. Their husbands don't respond when called. And they don't remember what their wives tell them.

The other day I told Jack I was going to a noon yoga class.

"What time?" he asked.

I actually sent him to a doctor to have his ears examined, and the doctor told him that his hearing is fine – it's his listening that's the problem.

The memory starts to go about the same time – for women as well as men. The names of people, cities, book titles simply disappear. Conversations start to sound like this:

"He looks just like... who's that famous actor? The one who made that movie with Barbara Streisand."

"I love that movie. Didn't he win an Oscar for the one about Africa?"

"ROBERT REDFORD!"

In our later years, Jack and I seem to have only one brain between us. He'll recall the song "Good Golly, Miss Molly." But I'll be the one to remember "Little Richard."

Or maybe we're both stuck on the original host of "Jeopardy." I might say that the last name began with an "F," which helps him come up with "Fleming... Art Fleming!"

Alone, we suffer from senior amnesia, also known as CRS (Can't Remember Shit). Together we have total recall.

CHAPTER 23

THE PREVENTIVE MAINTENANCE PAYOFF

So far, we've been talking about how to select a husband and how to maintain him in good working order. Now I want to discuss the benefits of doing so.

To begin with, there's something very satisfying about sharing your entire adult life with the same person – all the highs as well as all the lows.

All those images in your photo album. There you are together starting out as babies, then having babies of your own. Going from skinny to not-so-skinny. All the milestones and occasions – celebration after celebration, holiday after holiday, vacation after vacation – the same person at your side as the days blend into decades. Going grayer with the years, or in my case, getting blonder. There's something special about that.

But there's more. Remember those wedding vows we talked about earlier – when the bride and groom pledge to love each other for better or worse, for richer or poorer? Remember?

Well – surprise! – the good stuff actually comes later. If you can stick it out until after the kids are through school and the mortgage is paid off, the good part of marriage unfolds. You have more financial security and fewer demands on your time. You have more leisure. You can travel or pursue your hobbies or go on a yoga retreat. And you have someone who's willing to do it with you or, at least, pick you up at the airport after you've been rafting down the Amazon, climbing Kilimanjaro or visiting your sister in Toledo.

Karl Pillemer, a gerontologist at Cornell University who studied 700 elderly people for his book "30 Lessons for Loving," reports that 100 percent said that a long marriage was the best thing in their lives but that same 100 percent also said that marriage is hard – or that it's really, *really* hard.

I don't want to imply that being married is better than being single. Single has some pretty strong advantages as well:

1. You don't have to arm-wrestle for the remote control.
2. The toilet seat is always down.
3. You'll never be humiliated by someone texting his private parts over the internet.

On the other hand, if you're willing to put up with a few petty annoyances, a long-term marriage has its compensation.

TIME Magazine did a June 13, 2016, cover story on "How to Stay Married and Why." In it, author Belinda Luscombe reports: "Married people have better health, wealth and even better sex lives than singles, and will probably die happier."

My final advice, if you do want to stay married for the rest of your life: Pick the *right* guy in the first place, then nurture him as best you can, protecting his ego whenever possible. I think you'll find, as I have, that it's well worth it. And, for the love of God, stay away from professional athletes.

Customer Service Call

Judi: *Technical Support, may I help you?*

Caller: *Remember me? I called you earlier about my boyfriend who didn't want to talk about marriage.*

Judi: *Yes, of course.*

Caller: *I just wanted you to know that I'm engaged.*

Judi: *I'll send you my manual.*

ACKNOWLEDGMENTS

Cheryl Lavin Rapp, editor and funny lady

Sari Steinberg, proof reader and great audience

Plus all my friends who were so generous with their advice, counsel and stories about men.

Bobbi Baehne

Joan Beugen

Helen Bloch

Janet Ullrich Books

Pat Christenson

Sharon Sultan Cutler

Kelly Epperson

Stacy Derby

Dyana Flanigan

Marsha Goldstein

Erin Kelly Herrera

Judy Horwitz

Joan Kohn

Marilyn Liss

Phyllis Malitz

Julie Mitre

Kathy Ochab

Julie Paradise

Megan Robinson

Ann Cone Sevi

Jennifer Wolfe

Gail Zelitzky

For my mother, Rosalie Cone, who informed me that all men fart in bed.

And Jack Schindler, the love of my life, without whom none of this would be possible.